Through Desert's Fire

Through Desert's Fire

Carroll Blair

Aveon Publishing Company

ISBN: 978-1-936430-48-2

Library of Congress Control Number
2011903220

Aveon Publishing Co.
P.O. Box 380739
Cambridge, MA 02238-0739 USA

Also by Carroll Blair

Grains of Thought
Facing the Circle
Reel to Real
Shifting Tides
Reaches
Out of Silence
Quarter Notes
By Rays of Light
Into the Inner Life
Gnosis of the Heart
Soul Reflections
Beneath and Beyond the Surface
Of Courage and Commitment
For Today and Tomorrow
In Meditation
Sightings Along the Journey
Offerings to Pilgrims
Human Natures
(Of Animal and Spiritual)
Atoms from the Suns of Solitude
Colors of Devotion
Voicings
Through the Shadows
As the World Winds Flow

Do you know when change
is most in order? When things
get too comfortable, when
you feel too peaceful as
when a lullaby can put you
to sleep . . . the spirit like
the mind does not sleep
it needs the motion of fierce
winds, the challenge of fire to
sustain its light, to keep you
alert, to keep you on the path,
to keep you in the light.

The way to truth is not a race.
It doesn't care for sleep-runners;
it requires a pace that allows for
the many pains to be felt and
lessons to be learned on the
way to its discovery.

Before anything of substance
is learned, is created, one must
be forged in spiritual fire
one way or another.

The true seekers are humble,
unassuming, but their heart is
not of the sheep, but of the lion.

A gift of getting to the other side of a challenge is an even greater challenge that awaits.

It is by way of ordeal that
the way to the real is found.

The spiritual demands the
highest price for its treasure,
but it holds the highest treasure.

They learn most about the
center who venture to
the farthest edge.

The enlightened life longs for
the demise of all that bars the
way to further enlightenment,
to greater life.

Ever lighting, burning,
purifying is the heart
of the spiritual.

Rarer than the eye, the
ear, the mind for truth
is the courage.

To be fearful of pain
is to be fearful of growth.

The way to bliss is
not by way of bliss.

Wholeness of Being cannot
be achieved without
shatterings of being.

Fraternity initiations — gang
initiations — all child's play
compared to the initiations
into the higher regions
of the spiritual.

It is suffering that opens the
spirit, that deepens the spirit,
that wings the spirit,
rising into light.

To draw close to the light
is to draw near to the flame.

In every moment death
and resurrection awaits.

There are spiritual deaths,
but no spiritual Death, and
beyond spiritual Birth
there are endless births.

The cry of birth is the cry
of creation — (and so much
more when of the spiritual).

Before it gives profoundly
the spiritual takes away.

The desert is not a place to
find oneself, but to lose oneself.

It is the breaking down of "I"
that allows for transcendence.

As ego is being destroyed
life is being created.

Pain is the caterpillar that
transforms into the butterfly,
but only when it is borne.

What is bravely
endured turns to joy.

Hurt may come from spiritual
suffering, but never harm.

Never does a thorn hurt
more, or from it does one
bleed more than when
it is removed.

The pains of the spiritual
can be harsh, yet more
joy do they seed than any
comforts of the fleeting.

To experience what the spiritual
has to offer, one must open with
surrender to the experience.

How can one begin to be
spiritualized until being purged
of what is inimical to the divine?

If a stone could feel would it not
wince from the hammer-blows
of the sculptor? And a nature
that is being transformed into
something better — more noble
and beautiful . . . could this occur
without the blows of sufferings?

The wound is at the
center of healing.

It requires wisdom to know
how great a gift suffering
can be, and suffering to
acquire the wisdom.

Though ever loving, a
tougher love there is not
than that of the sacred.

The suffering of a higher
nature is a baptism
into higher nature.

Great joy is there in the matrix of ordeal when striving for something noble.

Nobility of spirit is not
only about creation, but
also destruction — i.e., the
destruction of ego.

One does not *live* who
knows of no other death
than that of the physical.

An awakening is born to,
but is also died to.

To grow spiritually is to
experience many spiritual
births and deaths.

When death occurs in the spiritual it is not followed by darkness, but even greater light.

Hints never cease of what is
needed for the fulfillment
of higher growth.

Suffering is the pregnancy
most often aborted because of
fear to see it through.

For the spirit of forbearance
suffering turns weakness to
strength, folly to wisdom,
and hatred to love.

As a suffering dies it leaves
in its wake an increase of
strength to add to the strength
that had endured.

The promise of life cannot
be realized in all its beauty
and profundity without
knowing what is beyond the
pain — only to be known
by going through it.

Before the ground brings forth
the flower it is scorched by
sun and beaten by rain.

It is after the storm, not before
that the rainbow appears.

The best of Life's poetry is
volatile, not serene; it explodes,
not soothes; it strikes its way to
the depths of Soul where the
best of Life's offerings await.

What breaks, opens, clearing
the way for something deeper
and more remarkable
to be revealed.

A continuum of breakthroughs
moving to the core of eternal being
is the spiritual quest.

Enlightenment refuses no one
who has made the journey to it,
nor carries anyone to the
stations of its light.

Spirituality is not a sanctuary
from ordeal, but the realm
in which all that could be
envisioned and internally
experienced within human
possibility can be realized.

Sooner or later Life confronts
everyone with having to decide
if one really wants the best
of what it has to give, and if
one is willing to pay the price.

The challenge of growth over
ease and comfort will always be
the choice of the noble spirit.

As essential as learning
to the realization of greater
life is the willingness to
engage the difficult.

From the pain that is faced
will beauty always rise.

The greatest of life is full of joy,
yet is not rooted in pleasures.

More than an aimless pleasure
will a directed suffering
bring benefit to the soul.

Spiritual suffering destroys
what needs to be destroyed to
strengthen and protect what is good
and create space for the flourishing
of more and greater good.

To not know spiritual suffering
is to not know spiritual love.

How can a life be anything but
cold or lukewarm that has
never gone to the flame?

One fears not the heat when
the spiritual is dancing within.

The suffering of a spiritual
nature breathes through the
heart of the sacred.

Spiritually speaking many
have not died enough
because they have not
suffered enough, and have
not suffered enough because
they have not lived enough.

Light is never so bright
as when it burns.

To live more is to exist less.

For the next birth does the
enlightened spirit ever yearn.

Without annihilation
transcendence cannot progress.

To die many times in life
is to know death's defeat.

There is always room for
another death, another birth
in the life of a great spirit.

The paradox of the true
individual is that one gives
his or her life over to Life —
brave enough to let go,
giving to Life, for Life.

Through courage and awareness,
not fear and sloth must the
surrender be to Life.

Time and again must destruction
be accepted into the life of
ever-growing creation.

With each transcendence
something remains from the
previous state that is carried
over to the next, something
that cannot be destroyed
which is essential to
the rising of future
states of being.

One cannot choose the time
of one's physical birth, or a
mother determine the precise
moment that she will bring
forth her child — and so with
spiritual birth . . . one neither
controls the time of birth
nor the nature of what
is being born.

The spiritual will always
deliver what one has earned.

The light, the Source is
through the pain, beaming
the story of bliss.

To turn from suffering is to also turn away from its gifts.

The great suffering brings the great tempest, the great repose, the great disturbance, the great silence, the great wisdom.

The prodigal son left what he knew with wealth, squandered it on ephemeral pleasures, and returned with nothing. The prophets left what they knew with nothing, endured ordeal after ordeal, and returned with great spiritual wealth.

One may drown in an
ocean of pleasures, yet find
treasure after treasure
in a desert of pain.

Within spiritual trial
lies the direction to freedom
and salvation.

Who is willing to give
everything is offered access
to all that the spiritual
has to give.

In the highest deliverance
joy and suffering meet at their
highest intensities and coalesce.

All saints have known the
ecstasy of dancing in the flame.

To come to life is to go to Life.

The gift of Life is dishonored
when its invitation to something
more than temporality is ignored.

Beyond quantifying is the difference between the life that is lived as a miscellany of experiences, and the life that is lived as an Experience.

A nature may enter the flame
as bronze and turn to gold.

To get through something in
the higher elevations of the
spiritual a stage of maturity
must be reached where there is
no longer a fervency to surmount
it, no longer a need to flatter
an ego that something difficult
has been overcome.

It is ego that exiles human
life from the eternal.

The aim of the spiritual is
not the preservation of "I,"
but its annihilation.

The vengeful of heart delight
in dancing on another's grave;
the enlightened delight
in dancing on their own.

When ego breaks it presents
the illusion that it is a break
of spirit, but it is the first of
many risings of the
power of spirit.

As a dust storm is the workings
of ego on the life it controls,
keeping from sight the
wonder that lies beyond it.

In the letting go is where
one is able to discover.

The enlightened strive to
create and to give, not to covet.

The spiritual is not only
drawn from, but also delivered
to in the advanced stages
of enlightenment.

What is pure can only
be approached with a
purity of heart.

To achieve a life of spiritual
truth lived in human form
is the great challenge
of human life.

Who turn to love cannot
fail to find courage.

With love and courage
wisdom is made possible.

In the spiritual is where
the principal force of human
entity is discovered, and
not by playing it safe.

To grow through the spiritual
is to work toward the trans-
formation of wounds of heart
and spirit into diamonds
of heart and spirit.

One must be the agent
of one's salvation.

In the spiritual one is both
the hunter and the hunted.

The right direction is the
same for all, but the right
path is reserved for only one.

Nowhere but downward
does the easy road go.

There will be no magic wand
to wake humankind to the
sacred power of Life — this,
to be achieved by the individual,
having the choice if he or she
will face what needs to be faced,
endure what needs to be endured
to earn the light of awakening.

Life is waiting for you, not
waiting on you — will you
let it teach you let it test you
let it awe and inspire you and
also confound you, and bring
joy and sorrow to you and
sometimes kill you to
bring forth another you
[a better you] . . . .
will you?

No matter what ordeals or
tribulations arise, Life is ever
pointing the way to love.

Does the spirit dance?   Yes.
          Does it sing?   Yes.
          Does it laugh?   Yes.
          Does it weep?   Yes.
          Does it pain?   Yes.
Does it rejoice?   Yes . . .
     in the miracle upon miracle
               that is Life.

ABOUT THE AUTHOR

Carroll Blair is an author of more than twenty books and the recipient of numerous awards. His work has been well endorsed and commendably reviewed. Among his titles cited for distinction are *Facing the Circle*, winner of the Pacific Book Awards, and *Quarter Notes*, winner of the Sharp Writ Book Awards. He is an alumnus of the Boston Conservatory and lives in Massachusetts.

www.ingramcontent.com/pod-product-compliance
Lightning Source LLC
Chambersburg PA
CBHW021159020426
42331CB00003B/135